Harriet Tubman

THE ROAD TO FREEDOM

Harriet Tubman
THE ROAD TO FREEDOM

by Rae Bains
illustrated by Larry Johnson

Troll Associates

Library of Congress Cataloging in Publication Data

Bains, Rae.
    Harriet Tubman, the road to freedom.

    Summary: The biography of a slave whose
flight to freedom was the first step in her
becoming a ''conductor'' on the underground
railroad.
    1. Tubman, Harriet, 1815?-1913—Juvenile
literature.   2. Underground railroad—Juvenile
literature.   3. Slaves—United States—Biography—Juvenile literature.   4. Afro-Americans
—Biography—Juvenile literature.   [1. Tubman,
Harriet, 1815?-1913.   2. Underground railroad.
3. Slaves.   4. Afro-Americans—Biography]
I. Johnson, Larry, 1949-   , ill.   II. Title.
E444.T82B34   973′0496073024 [B] [92]   81-23145
ISBN 0-89375-760-8   AACR2
ISBN 0-89375-761-6 (pbk.)

10   9   8   7   6   5   4   3

Harriet Tubman

THE ROAD TO FREEDOM

It was beautiful along the eastern shore of Maryland's Chesapeake Bay. The waters were filled with fish, oysters, and clams. In the woods lived rabbits, woodchucks, muskrats, deer, and squirrels. Corn, tobacco, wheat, and vegetables grew in the rich soil.

Maryland was a fine place to live during the early 1800s—if you were free. Ben Ross and Harriet Green were not. They were the slaves of a plantation owner named Edward Brodas. They worked in his fields, cut his lumber, and were his house servants. They did anything he ordered them to do. And their children did the same.

7

Slaves were called "chattel." That meant they were pieces of property, like sheep or furniture or bales of cotton. The slaves knew that they could be sold at any time. They knew that their children could be taken from them and sent far, far away, and that they could be beaten or whipped. And they knew that their masters would never be punished. For slaves had no rights. They were not allowed any kind of education; they were not even allowed to attend church.

This was the sort of world into which Harriet Ross was born, around 1820. She was the sixth of eleven children born to Ben Ross and Harriet Green. They all lived in a tiny, one-room shack. It had a dirt floor, no windows, and no furniture.

There were no beds. The whole family slept on rags and straw spread on the floor. There were no dishes. The slaves' food—mostly corn mush—was eaten right from the pot it was cooked in. They would scoop it out with a piece

of flat stone or an oyster shell. And when they
ate, they had to stand or sit on the hard ground.

Slave children had almost no time to play.
They were put to work as soon as possible, to
"earn their keep." When Harriet was still a very
small child, she began running errands for Mr.
Brodas and his family. She carried messages as
far as ten miles away. She had to go over back
roads, through woods, and along river banks.

The only tenderness in Harriet's life came from her family. They gave her so much love that she always had something wonderful to hold on to, even at the worst of times. And one day—many years later—Harriet would thank her parents in the best way she could. She would rescue them, plus six of her brothers and one sister, from slavery, taking them north to freedom.

Soon after she turned five, Harriet was given a new task. Mrs. Brodas put her to work in the mansion, called the "big house." The little girl didn't know a thing about housework. She had never even been inside a real house before—only in the one-room slave shacks. And to make things worse, nobody showed her how to do the things she was supposed to do in the mansion.

So it was no surprise when Harriet made all kinds of mistakes. And when she made mistakes, she was punished.

When Harriet was six, she was sent to live with a family named Cook. They were weavers. Their home was many miles from the Brodas plantation. Harriet hated being so far from her family. But the Brodases wanted her to learn weaving. Then she would be able to weave for the Brodas family. So, like it or not, Harriet went.

Life with the Cooks was no better than it had been on the Brodas plantation. But Harriet did not stay with the Cooks long. One day, even though she was very sick with measles, Mr. Cook sent her down to the river. She was told to check his muskrat traps. To do this, she had to wade through ice-cold, fast-flowing waters.

The next day, Harriet began to shake and cough. Soon she was burning with fever and could not do any work. She lay in a corner, feeling terrible. Word of her illness quickly passed from one slave to the next, until it reached Harriet's mother.

She begged Mr. Brodas to bring her little girl home. Mr. Brodas agreed. He didn't want to pay the Cooks for teaching someone who was too sick to learn anything. So he had Harriet brought home. There, her mother nursed the little girl back to health.

Harriet's next job was looking after Mrs. Brodas's baby. Here is how Harriet talked about it years later. "I was only seven years old when I was sent to take care of the baby. I was so little I had to sit on the floor and have the baby put in my lap. And that baby was always in my lap except when it was asleep or its mother was feeding it."

Handling such a big responsibility was hard for young Harriet. She never had any time to play or be by herself. She was constantly watched by Mr. and Mrs. Brodas, and they were very strict with her. If she misbehaved, Harriet knew she would be given a whipping. This kind of punishment was used all the time. The owners wanted to keep their slaves frightened.

They did not want the slaves to speak up or fight back—or try to escape.

But the owners could not break the spirit of the slaves. There always were slaves who stood up for their rights. They bravely held religious services, even though that was forbidden. They studied reading and writing in secret. They hid and fed other slaves who were trying to escape to the North.

And every year there were slave uprisings. The plantation owners tried to keep the news of these revolts from getting out. They didn't want their own slaves to hear of them. They might want to do the same thing. But word still passed from one slave to another, from one plantation to another all over the South. It didn't matter that the owners told each other—and the rest of the world—that the slaves were content. The slaves knew better.

From the time she was a baby, Harriet listened to the stories of slaves fighting back. She heard of a slave named Gabriel Prosser. In 1800, Prosser had planned a great rebellion. More than one thousand slaves were ready to march with him. But he was stopped at the last moment, when a traitor told several slave owners about the rebellion.

Harriet also heard of Denmark Vesey, who preached that all people were equal. Vesey was a free black man who had once been a slave. He was also the leader of thousands of slaves living in South Carolina. In June of 1822, Vesey's group was ready to rise up in the name of freedom. But his plans, like those of Gabriel Prosser, were told to slave owners by frightened servants.

Harriet heard of other uprisings—large and small—taking place in many parts of the South. All this meant one thing to the young girl—she was not the only angry slave in America. *Someday,* she told herself, *I'm going to be free! And*

when that day comes, I'm going to help bring others to freedom.

Harriet did not hide her feelings. She spoke out fearlessly to the other slaves on the plantation. And she refused to smile or make believe she was happy in front of the Brodas family.

Harriet's mother was worried about her. If Harriet angered Mr. Brodas or his wife, they might sell Harriet down the river. Selling someone down the river meant selling that person to a slave trader. The trader would take his new slave down to the Deep South to be put to work in the rice or cotton fields. Life was hard for a slave in Maryland. But it was ten times harder in the Deep South.

Mrs. Brodas did not like Harriet's proud, defiant looks. She decided to break the child's spirit. To do so, she hired out the nine-year-old girl to another family in the county. These people made her work all day, cleaning house.

Then she had to work at night, caring for a baby. For no reason she was punished every day. And she was fed only enough food to keep her alive.

After a while, Harriet was little more than skin and bones. She was not able to work anymore. Now, sure that she was "broken," the family sent Harriet back to the Brodas plantation. Her body *was* weak and weary, but not her spirit. That was still strong.

Harriet's parents did their best to help her get well. Her mother nursed her every free moment she had. And Ben taught her all kinds of amazing and useful things. Even though he had never gone to school, Ben was a very wise man. He knew a lot about nature. He could tell that it would be a hard winter when the animals grew thicker coats in the fall. He knew where the fishing was good. And he knew which wild plants were safe to eat. As soon as Harriet was up and about, he took her on Sunday-afternoon walks in the woods and along the river.

Part of Harriet's strength came from her brothers and sisters. After a day of working in the fields under a boiling sun, they came back to the shack. They brought her all the news of the day. They sang songs. They told stories. They told jokes to make her laugh. They did everything they could to make their little sister happy.

Another part of Harriet's strength came from her faith. The slaves were not allowed to have a real church. But they were very religious and held services every Sunday morning. On every plantation there usually was at least one slave who could read or knew the Bible very well. And from this person all the other slaves learned Bible stories and prayers.

Of all the stories in the Bible, the one the slaves liked most was about Moses. He had led the Israelites from slavery. The slaves prayed for a Moses of their own, someone who would lead them to freedom.

Harriet believed deeply that the burden on her people would be eased. She believed that they were meant to be free. She believed what the Bible said: that all people were equal in the eyes of God.

In the next three years, Harriet grew stronger in body and faith. As soon as she was completely well, Mr. Brodas hired her out to another master. This one had her do work hard enough for a grown man. She split rails with an axe, hauled wood, and did other heavy jobs. It was difficult but she never gave up, even when it seemed too much to bear.

By the time she was eleven, Harriet was muscular and very strong. She could work as hard and as long as any grownup. Mr. Brodas saw this and put her to work in the fields. Like all the other women in the fields, Harriet wore a bandanna—a large handkerchief—on her head.

For the rest of her life she would always wear a bandanna. It was to remind her of her days as a slave, and how far from the fields she had come.

In 1831, new, harsher laws were passed. Now, slaves were not allowed to gather in groups. They were not supposed to talk while they worked. They were never to be on the public roads without a pass from their masters. And the old rules were made stricter. All of this happened because of an uprising led by a man named Nat Turner.

Nat Turner was a slave from Virginia. In the summer of 1831, this man—called the Prophet—led about seventy slaves in a bloody revolt. It took armed troops to stop the revolt and three full months to capture Turner.

The slave owners were scared. If a revolt could happen in Virginia, it could happen anywhere. This fear haunted them more and more. That is why they made stricter laws for the slaves.

But Nat Turner had lit the flame of freedom in many slaves. Harriet was one of these. "I feel just like Nat Turner did," she said one night to her family. "It's better to be dead than a slave."

"It's better to be alive and free," said her brother William.

"And how do we get that?" Harriet asked him. "You know Mr. Brodas won't ever give us our freedom."

"I'm not talking about what he gives," William told her. "I'm talking about what we take for ourselves—like a ride to freedom on the underground railroad."

"What's that?" Harriet wanted to know.

William told Harriet the story of Tice Davids. Mr. Davids was a slave in Kentucky who ran away. When the plantation owner found out that Davids was gone, he set out after him. Davids swam across the Ohio River with the owner rowing close behind. By the time the owner's boat landed, there was no trace of Tice Davids. It was as if he had vanished into thin air.

The runaway was being helped by people who hated slavery. But the plantation owner knew only that he had vanished. When the slave owner returned, he told everybody that "Tice Davids disappeared so fast, he must have gone on an underground road."

This story was repeated again and again. Soon slaves were talking about the wonderful secret passage to freedom. Of course, there was no underground road or tunnel from the South to the North. But the slaves kept telling the story anyway. It gave them hope.

Around this time the first railroads were being built in the United States. Trains were the fastest way of traveling that anyone had ever seen. The slaves heard about the railroads. Soon, people were talking about the "underground railroad" that took runaway slaves quickly and safely to the North.

The truth had nothing to do with trains and underground tunnels. The truth was that there were good people who risked their lives to help slaves escape. Some of them hid runaways in their cellars, barns, attics, or in secret rooms in their houses.

These brave people were called "station-masters." The hiding places were called "depots" or "stations." Other people took the runaways from one depot to another in a hay wagon, on horseback, or on foot. These people were called "conductors." The runaways themselves were known as "passengers" or "parcels." A child was a "small parcel," and a grownup was a "large parcel."

After William told Harriet about the underground railroad, she thought about it all the time. *Maybe*, she told herself, *I'll take that ride to freedom. Maybe all of us will.* It was this hope that kept Harriet going.

When Harriet was fifteen her hope—and her life—almost ended. One September evening she was sent to the village store. While she was there another slave hurried in. He belonged to a farmer named Barrett. A moment later Mr. Barrett rushed in.

"Get back to the field!" Barrett shouted at the slave.

The slave just stared back silently. Nobody else in the store made a move.

"I'll whip you," Barrett threatened.

The slave began to edge away. "Stop!" Barrett yelled.

"You," Barrett said, pointing at Harriet and a young boy next to her. "Hold him so I can tie him up."

Harriet didn't obey the order. And she kept the boy from doing anything.

Suddenly, the slave ran to the door. Barrett leaped to the store counter and picked up a heavy lead weight. He whirled and threw the weight at the runaway. But it missed the man.

The heavy piece of metal struck Harriet in the head. She fell to the floor, unconscious.

For the next couple of months Harriet lay near death. At first, she couldn't eat. She grew thinner and thinner. She slept most of the time. Her wound was healing slowly, but there was a very deep cut in her forehead. It left a scar she would carry for the rest of her life.

Mr. Brodas was sure Harriet was going to die. So he tried to sell her. Time after time he brought slave buyers to the shack, where Harriet lay on a pile of rags. But each time the buyer's answer was the same: "Even if she lives, she'll never be able to put in a day's work. I wouldn't give you a penny for her."

Winter came, and Harriet was still alive. Her parents were thankful but still worried about her. Harriet could walk and talk and do light chores around the shack. But sometimes, in the middle of whatever she was doing, Harriet fell asleep.

It could happen even while she was saying something. She would simply stop talking, close her eyes, and sleep for a few minutes. Then she would wake up and go on talking as if no time had passed.

The Brodas family was sure that Harriet's "spells" meant she was half-witted. So they tried that much harder to sell her. But Harriet did not want to be sold and sent away from her family. And she certainly was not half-witted. She was a very clever fifteen-year-old.

Every time Mr. Brodas came to the shack with a buyer, Harriet made believe that she was having one of her spells. Or she acted very, very stupid. Her family and friends went along with Harriet's play-acting. And nobody was ever interested in buying her.

In time, Harriet's strength returned. She could lift huge, heavy barrels. She could pull a loaded wagon for miles. She drove the oxen in the fields and plowed from morning to night. It was said that she was stronger than the strongest man in Maryland. It was a strength she would need in the days to come.

Harriet's dream of freedom was still alive. But she had to put it off for a while. In 1844, she married a free black man named John Tubman. She hoped that he would help her get away to the North. But the marriage was not happy, and they soon parted. Harriet continued to use the name of Tubman.

Not long after that, word reached the Brodas slaves that many of them were going to be sold. Harriet knew the time had come to make the break for freedom. She turned for help to a white woman who lived nearby. This woman had once told Harriet, "If you ever need anything, come to me." Harriet knew that meant helping her to escape.

Without telling anyone, Harriet set out for Bucktown, where the white woman lived. When she reached the house, Harriet said to the woman, "You told me to come when I needed your help. I need it now."

The woman gave Harriet a paper with two names on it, and directions how she might get to the first house where she would receive aid.

When Harriet reached this first house, she showed the woman of the house the paper. Harriet was told to take a broom and sweep the yard. In this way, anyone passing the house would not suspect the young woman working in the yard of being a runaway slave.

The woman's husband, who was a farmer, came home in the early evening. In the dark he loaded a wagon, put Harriet in it, well covered, and drove to the outskirts of another town. Here he told her to get out and directed her to a second "station."

Harriet was passed along this way, from station to station. She was riding the underground railroad, and she didn't stop until she crossed into Pennsylvania. Now she was free at last! As she remembered years later, "When I found I had crossed that line, I looked at my hands to see if I was the same person. There was such a glory over everything. The sun came like gold through the trees, and over the fields, and I felt like I was in heaven."

But Harriet's "heaven" wasn't perfect. "I was free," she said, "but there was no one to welcome me to the land of freedom. I was a

stranger in a strange land. And my home, after
all, was down in Maryland, because my father,
my mother, my brothers, my sisters, and friends
were there. But I was free, and they should be
free! I would make a home in the North and
bring them there."

In the next few years, Harriet did what she
swore she would do. She made trip after trip to
the South, risking her life to bring others to
freedom. She rescued her family, friends, other
slaves—more than three hundred men, women,
and children.

45

Harriet was loved by the slaves. They called her their "Moses," because she led them through the wilderness and out of bondage. And she was hated by the slave owners, who offered a $40,000 reward for her capture.

Harriet was never caught. She became the most famous conductor on the underground railroad. And, as she said, "I never ran my train off the track, and I never lost a passenger."

The legend of Harriet Tubman grew during the Civil War. Fighting for the Union, she made many raids behind enemy lines as a scout and a spy. And as a nurse, she helped the sick and wounded soldiers, both Northerners and Southerners.

After the Civil War, Harriet made her home in Auburn, New York. But she never stopped doing good works. Until her death, on March 10, 1913, the woman called Moses did many things. She fought for the right of women to vote. She helped create schools for black students. She did everything she could for the poor, the old, and the helpless.

When Harriet Tubman died, at the age of
ninety-three, she was honored with a military
funeral. It was a fitting tribute to the woman
who fought so many battles for the freedom of
her people.